FISH IN A BARREL

Nick Cave & The Bad Seeds On Tour

by Peter Milne

Introduction by Nick Cave

Introduction

"Peter Milne is an unbelievably malicious photographer. He calls himself a voyeur, which I find rather extraordinary because he's anything but a voyeur. He consciously takes control of situations, bends them out of shape, pits people against each other and then photographs the aftermath.

Peter sees himself as one who sits on the periphery of the activity of his subjects and photographs them in their different situations. But a voyeur doesn't, for example, go up to a person who's fallen into a drunken coma and snap photographs with the flash right in front of their eyes in order to wake them up, just to capture their expression of horror and panic; a voyeur doesn't pretend to be the house cleaner and come into your bedroom at 6 a.m. to take photographs of you in bed.

He's basically interested in people's suffering. He only likes taking photographs of people when they don't want to have their photograph taken, which excites him, and that's how he sees his role as a photographer. He's an extremely nice person but as a photographer he's almost unbearable.

Peter Milne is interested in you at your most run-down, crapulent, bloated self, and of course that's what makes for the best photographs. Everyone likes to see a bit of decay. I think he's a brilliant photographer; he has enormous stamina and he's interested in his job from the moment he wakes up to the moment he goes to sleep, but for that reason it is often excruciating to have him around.

He's a very sensitive sort of person, but he puts his work before anything else - he's a true artist in that respect. Whenever he walks into a room, camera around his neck, there's always a unanimous 'Oh God, no...' and still he strides in. If you tell him to go away he doesn't. Everyone tells him to go away all the time but he just doesn't. I've seen him get punched, and even then he continued to snap away to capture the flying fist on film.

As a friend who I've known for many, many years, he's a different person when he puts his camera down. He relaxes and softens. I think he thinks it's necessary to behave the way he does in order to promote certain reactions in people. In some of his photographs where people look angry or bored or irritated, it's often because of him. Because of his flashing and snapping. Even though he was with us so much that we tended to forget about him after a while, there was always this annoying little clicking sound in the background.

When I first met him, which was around the time of the punk days in Melbourne, he was one of the only people I knew who wasn't a raging alcoholic or drug addict. In fact he didn't take any drugs or drink at all. But he exhibited the most alarming behaviour for one who was clean and sober. He used to carry a staple gun around with him all the time and shoot staples into his arm constantly. He would just walk up to you - bang bang, staple in the arm - and grin.

He's taken photographs of me and my friends right from the start. Any opportunity he has to be within our presence, he's taken photographs. So I've always known him as someone who just takes photographs all the time. Once I asked him how he knew he was getting good photographs, and he told me it was a case of knowing when the time was right. That, he said, was his talent - an intuitive feeling.

He doesn't wait for things to happen; if he's in some kind of social situation and the time is right, then he puts the camera up to his face and looks through it as if it were an eye, and off he goes, shooting fish in a barrel. He just wanders around the room with this thing on his face, moving from side to side, and he sees things and starts clicking. And he suddenly knows when it's going well: he gets this feeling every time he clicks that it's something amazing. That's pretty interesting, I think.

He used to be a practical joker. He has a very irreverent sense of humour and his photography is an extension of an infantile, malicious schoolboy streak that he has. I remember picking up a girl at a party once; I was sitting on the floor talking to her, and when we tried to leave I found I couldn't stand up because Peter had stapled my jacket to the floor. I got really pissed off with him and said if he ever did that again I'd break his staple gun, and I took my jacket off and had to go and re-get the girl and start all over again. When I left, my jacket had been stapled to the ceiling. He's a real child. He even looks like an overgrown child.

I think his photography must be an extension of his relentless curiosity. He always asks questions. You can imagine how annoying it was to have a person on tour that's constantly trying to find out about you, constantly provoking you in order to get a good photograph, and constantly, relentlessly and without ever any intention of stopping, snapping your photograph. But I have great respect for that, because he's good, apart from anything else. He's really good, so it's worthwhile.

Different members of the group tolerated it to different extents. Blixa is used to being photographed all the time, and therefore it doesn't affect him at all, he's detached from it. I think Conway and Martin were intensely annoyed by it. Thomas doesn't mind because he always looks good, as if he's just been dry-cleaned. Mick raised his eyebrows a few times. But for me, it's a painful process because I hate having my photograph taken. It means that I'm always having to be reminded of myself and the way I am and the way I look. I don't mind seeing the finished photographs, but when I hear the camera go off I can't help but be aware of the sort of person I am.

Peter is a very brave photographer because he involves himself in situations where he knows he's not welcome. He's also putting himself on the line with his friends; it's not as if he's photographing people he doesn't care about. He cares what we think about him and whether or not we like him, but in the end we're very protective of Peter. Our standard introduction to people when we arrived in a new city was 'Hi, I'm Nick Cave, and this is the Bad Seeds and this is Peter Milne – be nice to him. Tolerate him.'

Although we don't like being photographed, we have come to terms with the less attractive aspects of our personalities, and don't mind them being documented. In the end what Peter managed to get was a truly accurate account of what it was like to be with the Bad Seeds on that particular tour last year.

I like his photographs a lot because he's interested in people in the same way as I am. He's interested in extremes. He likes his subjects to be angry or bored or exhausted or sad or drunk. Although when I think about it, he's far more interested in people who are hungover than people who are drunk. He's comfortable with the uncomfortable. ”

Nick Cave
London, 1993

Japan

TOKYO

TOKYO

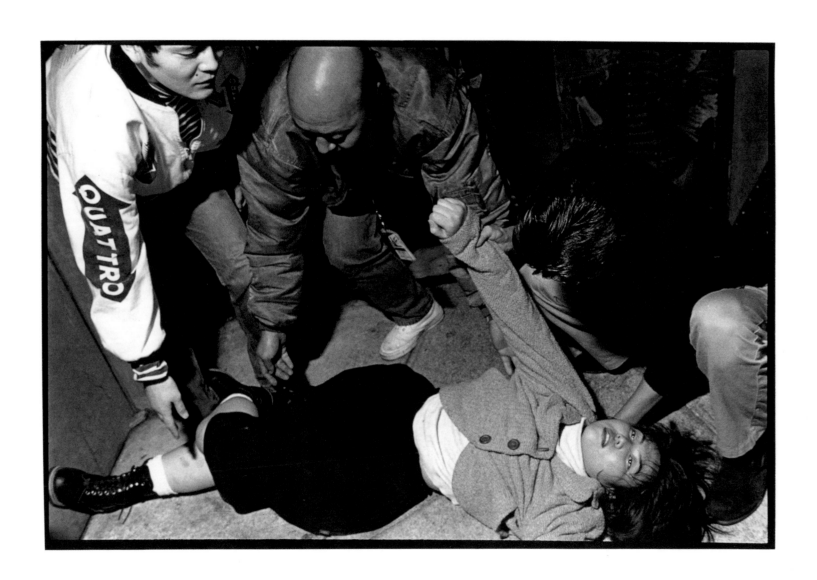

NAGOYA

TOKYO

BULLET TRAIN
Tour Manager

BULLET TRAIN

Commuting Businessman #1

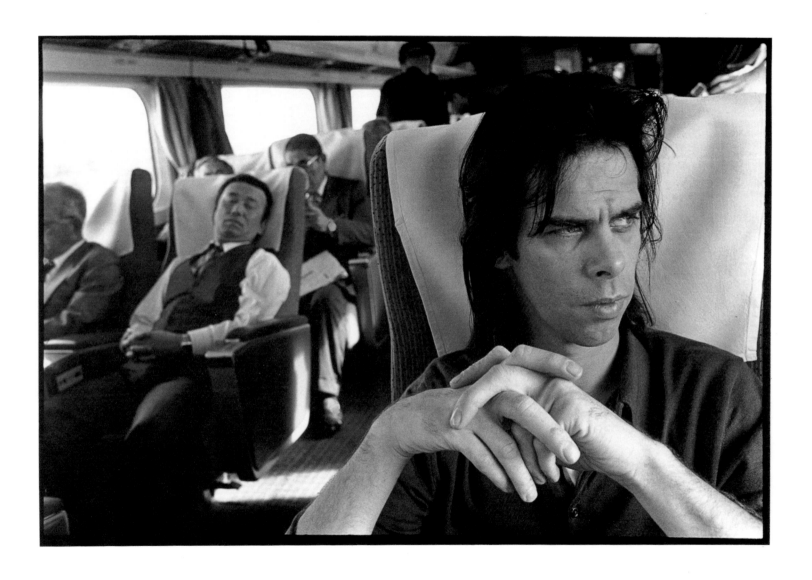

TOKYOBULLET TRAIN

Commuting Businessman #2

FUKUOKA

NAGOYA

OSAKA

OSAKA

TOKYO

TOKYO

TOKYO

The handwritten setlist in the photograph reads:

JACK the RIPPER
ETERNITY
The MERCY SEAT
SHIP SONG
RAINY NIGHT in SOHO
DEANNA
DREAM
HENRY
BROTHER JOE
TUPELO
LUCY
NEW MORNING
The CARNY
CHRISTINA
The GOOD SON
WEEPING SONG
... TIME MAN
... ME TO TOWN
... IS OVER
... in G.

BLACK BETTY
I WANNA BE DOG
PROUD MARY

FUKUOKA

TOKYO

TOKYO

TOKYO

CLUB QUATTRO

CLUB QUATTRO

CLUB QUATTRO

FUKUOKA

Mixing "Henry's Dream"
Melbourne, Australia

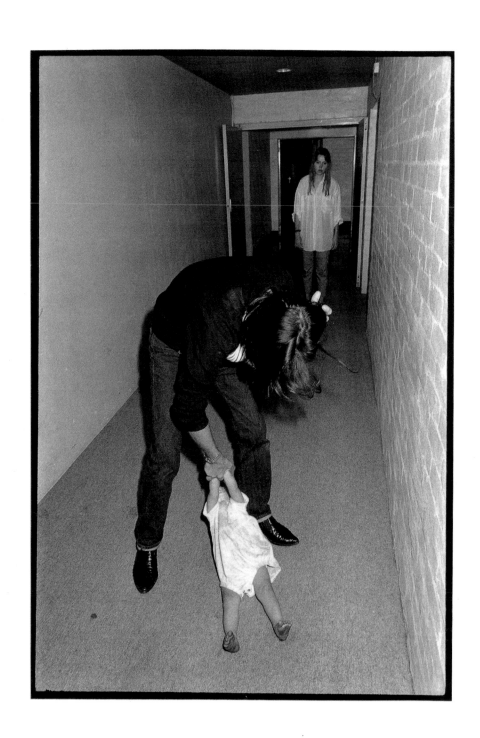

BRADFORD

Europe

AUTOBAHN – GERMANY

PARIS

KÖLN

MUNICH

MUNICH

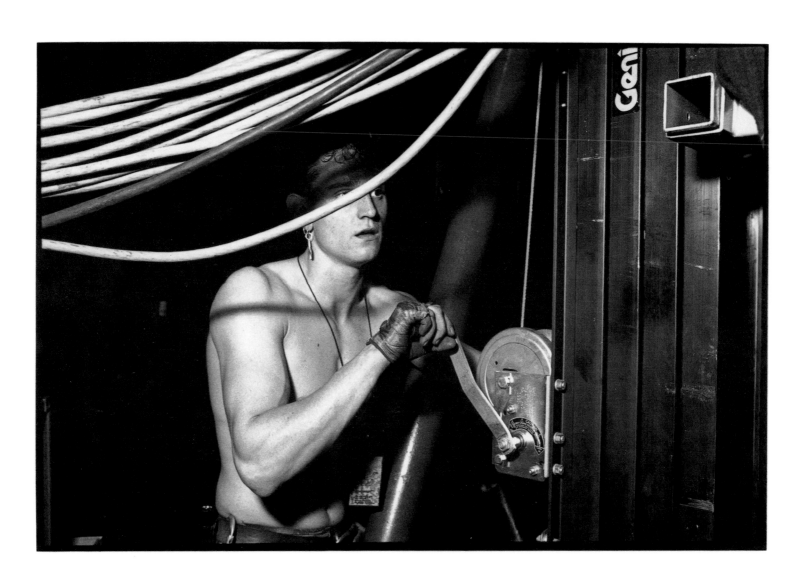

MUNICH

GHENT – BELGIUM

KÖLN

HAMBURG

HAMBURG

HAMBURG

PARIS

BERLIN
X.N.Pop Nightclub

Australia

SYDNEY

MELBOURNE

MELBOURNE

MELBOURNE

MELBOURNE

SYDNEY

SYDNEY

CANBERRA

ADELAIDE

ADELAIDE

MELBOURNE

MELBOURNE

MELBOURNE

Nick Cave talking to Peter Milne

PM: The tour of Europe with the Bad Seeds was one of the greatest adventures of my life. It wouldn't be true to say that I enjoyed every moment of it, but it was an amazing adventure and as a photographer it was an incredible opportunity. Sometimes there was so much happening that I just had to point the camera in any direction and something interesting would occur. It wasn't until quite late in the tour that the idea of doing a book was seriously discussed; early on my reason for being there was pretty tenuous – I just sort of invited myself along.

NC:We liked your photographs, and the photos you'd taken in the studio of us.

Yeah, but there was nothing concrete. It was Rayner who suggested the possibility of a book. From that moment on I felt a pressure I hadn't felt earlier. Some bits of it – Milan was a notable example – were just a big party; getting pissed and touring round Europe in a bus with all these boys.

So you enjoyed it because you could participate safely in it; it wasn't your entire life. You could just enter it for a while, snap away and walk out the other side.

Yes, but I think I enjoyed it because for everybody involved, not just for me, it's not quite the real world, is it?

Isn't it?

PM: Well is it? In the midst of all of that you really try and hold on to some semblance of reality. There was a macho kind of atmosphere that sometimes occurs when it's just the boys out on tour, which I occasionally found quite threatening. I was often the butt of excessive amounts of affectionate teasing from the boys. There were moments on that tour when I was in an emotionally vulnerable state, I can't remember why, times when I really felt like I needed a bit of support from those around me, and I received it more when you had your girlfriends along. Of course, the down side of that was there weren't so many drunken football matches in hotel rooms which are such a rich source of photographic imagery...

You must expect that sort of reaction to you sometimes, having the job that you have.

Yeah, and I admit that sometimes I was really bloody obnoxious.

You're an enormously obnoxious photographer. I always felt that you saw being offensive as part and parcel of being a photographer; that you have to be like that in order to create your photographs. Otherwise you'd be creating something lesser. You

can be relentlessly irritating
with the camera - you go into a
situation where nobody wants to
be photographed, which is when
you like taking photographs the
most, and constantly snap away,
despite the fact that you're
getting extremely hostile
vibrations. Sometimes, people
even say to you: 'Peter - stop
taking photographs...' and still
you just snap gladly away. You're
putting yourself into a situation
where you are an irritant.

I like the sound of that. I'm hesitant to argue
against something which is shaping up to be
such a nice bit of mythologising. I really like
the sound of being obnoxious. I really like
the stigma of the kind of negative glamour of
that. But when all is said and done, if I'm
photographing people who I respect and
admire - and the Bad Seeds fit into that
category - I don't think I'm trying to do a
hatchet job.

No, that's not what I'm saying at
all. I know you're not trying to
take pictures of us to
incriminate us in any way. I just
think that sometimes you are
deliberately annoying in order to
provoke certain situations.

I think sometimes I am...

Well you are. You know that you
are.

This is part of why this whole experience was
a bit of an Epiphany for me, because by the
end of it I realised that I was finding my
niche. The whole Bad Seeds thing has turned
into a huge project - with the exhibitions,
and now the book - which is obviously very
important for me. But I honestly think,
especially early on, that I wasn't aware I was
deliberately being irritating. And if it doesn't
come across as sounding very stupid, I'd like
to pay tribute to how tolerant I thought you
all were.

All of those pictures were taken
with a lot of love and fondness,
I think, and that comes through
very clearly.

I would like to think that they were taken
with a sense of humour, too, and that they
reflect the sense of humour of their subjects.
We're sympatico, aren't we?

More or less. Peter, as a young
man you were a great practical
joker with a distinctly malicious
aspect to your pranks. Do you
think that having a camera gives
you a license to indulge this
malicious and ultimately
adolescent side of your
personality?

Absolutely, absolutely. Clearly, unequivocally, yes. One of the things I love about photography is that it's a great vehicle for a voyeur, because it gives you an excuse to hang around. One of the advantages of being a photographer is that it's an excuse to be an observer – to watch something for no reason other than being interested in watching it. If I'd rang Mick Harvey and said 'Hey, you're touring Europe, I'd really like to come along and hang around and be obnoxious,' I don't think I would have got a very warm response. But my camera gave me a foot in the door.

If you'd gone without your camera wouldn't you have felt very frustrated?

Of course. I would have felt useless. But it's true that I use my camera to take me into situations that I want to observe, and which would otherwise not be open to me.

How much do you respect people if they beg you not to photograph them?

I do respect them. I might push it and get it down on film, but as most people will tell you, if anybody expresses a sincere abhorrence to a particular image of them, then I'm quite happy to tear it up.

But you don't like having your

own photograph taken, right?

Right. I've taught myself to tolerate it, because I feel like such a hypocrite. But hardly anybody likes it, and I don't like people who enjoy having their photo taken. I'm immediately suspicious that they might not have an entirely healthy attitude to the whole business of their self-image. I hate having my own photograph taken, but these days I've taught myself, if somebody points a camera at me, to try and relax and just accept it. But I'm never happy with the result. I don't look the way I'd like to look. But I love being interviewed.

That makes me a bit suspicious. Are there any limits that you wouldn't transgress for a picture?

Absolutely. I concede the point about what a bully I am, but I definitely have scruples. I wouldn't put something in an exhibition or a book if I felt it was going to hurt somebody that I have respect for.

It's the taking of the photo that's the actual invasion, not the result.

That's an interesting distinction. I think that the photograph doesn't become a reality until it's put into a finished form. All photography really comes down to –

when you take away the little bit of technique that's involved, which is really not of any great consequence – is a process of selection. When you aim the camera you're selecting one image over another, just as you are in the darkroom when you look at a contact sheet and decide to print one image over another. And I do sometimes hold back. I was being commissioned by GQ magazine in Japan, so it was different, but lots of those photos in Europe, especially early on, were taken when I was drunk. It was either just before a gig or during a gig, or just after a gig. The whole thing was a bit of a party for me, and in that sort of situation I don't have a lot of scruples, and if I did start to have some, I'd probably think to myself, 'Oh well, bugger it, I'll worry about it in the darkroom when it comes to printing.' But in a normal situation, I do have scruples. Maybe my manner is such that my scruples are not immediately apparent to the people that I'm thrusting a camera at.

Were you more restrained in Japan? You worked much harder, and you were much more of a bully, making us get up early in the morning and do things.

You mean when I photographed you naked in bed? I knew the girls would go for it. I must say I was a bit disappointed with the girl situation. I was up for action, but I just didn't get any offers. I had dreams that there would be groupies en masse, and that the order would start with the band, then go down through the crew, and possibly I'd be able to get my name at the bottom of the list, but that I'd still have a choice of at least five or six girls. It wasn't the case at all. It was very slim pickings. That is one aspect of the tour that I found deeply disappointing.

I'm joking, of course.

Of course, Peter. Anyway, you couldn't really invite a girl back to your bus...

Exactly. It should be pointed out that my trip to Europe was done on virtually no money at all. I was sleeping on the bus, and there was a period of two weeks where I didn't have a single coin in my pocket, so all the meals I had were meals provided for the band. There were days when I only ate at the soundcheck, and if there wasn't a soundcheck, I ate absolutely nothing. So during this whole period I was living the life of a gypsy. But I'm not complaining – it was a free trip around Europe.

How did you get over there? Did we pay for that?

Good question. I must have paid for it, no, hang on. I don't know. I can't remember. My memory doesn't run to that kind of detail. I'm sure I borrowed it from someone.

No-one can remember anything when they come from Australia. So, ultimately, how do you see the Bad Seeds, having spent all that time with them?

OK, I'll say something that may sound so laudatory that you'll suspect my sincerity. It is a fair vindication of my faith in the Bad Seeds as a creative outfit that I walked away from the whole thing with more respect for the group as individuals, and more respect and admiration for the music that you produce. I thought you acquitted yourselves with distinction.

Mick Harvey can be a grouchy old bear, but he's one of the human beings I admire and respect most in the world, though sometimes I find him intimidating and scary. The only individual within the Bad Seeds that I've ever had any trouble with is Conway: it's a bit of a personality clash and I don't really think he likes me very much. That occasionally caused trouble in Europe, especially when he was very drunk. But by the time we got to Japan – after he and I flew over together, and he was incredibly pissed and really unpleasant to the poor JAL hostesses who really couldn't cope – we were quite chummy.

Ask me more questions. I love this, I'm just warming up. I'm hoping that by the time this book gets published in America, I'll be on **Donahue**.

How do you justify going on tour and photographing a group of musicians without having the slightest interest in music?

Fair question. It's not that I don't have the slightest interest in music. It's just I don't have a passionate interest in it, especially compared to most people I associate with, people to whom music is a deeply, deeply important part of life. I've never felt that kind of passion about it but it doesn't mean that I'm insensitive to the emotive power that music can have, and if there's any band that I do respond to warmly, it's the Bad Seeds. I absolutely love the music of the Bad Seeds, and it's one of the reasons I originally wanted to go on tour. The concerts are my fondest memories of it. There were several nights when I didn't even bother taking photographs, and yet I used my camera as an excuse to crawl into that no-man's land between the stage and the barrier, simply to be really close to the full sound and watch the whole show.

You were very encouraging actually. I remember being completely exhausted and looking down after a song and there you were, applauding away down the front, and it always gave me a lot of power.

That's a real revelation to me. I felt invisible,

and your attention was always focussed in the infinite distance.

Should we make a comment about the dynamics of the book? How Mick Harvey and Katy Beale and everybody involved arrived at the selection of the photographs? Or is that just too tedious?

I don't know. Sounds pretty bloody tedious to me. You can do it.

Well, I selected a pile of photos that I was really happy with – I think there were about 140. Mick and Katy then cut it down to about 110 and worked out the running order.

Let's look at the photographs. I like this one – particularly the spilt bits on Thomas' shirt and the look of religious ecstasy on Conway's face. What are we going to do about the captions?

I don't want to caption them. I thought some of the titles at your exhibition...

Sucked?

Yeah. I think we should just have the names of the cities and the dates.

I'm open to persuasion. Don't you like the homo-erotic quality of this one? There's quite a few with that homo-erotic quality. And this one says such a lot about the nature of pop stardom and fan adoration – the whole bit. And what about that one? Technically I don't think it passes muster.

Technically I can't comment.

This is one I slipped in with a question mark over it. I like it. It's taken in Victor's room. And this is a silly photo of you, let's junk it.

My body looks really nice in that, but my head looks horrible.

Well, I don't necessarily always want to make people look silly. If your body looks nice, I don't have a problem with that.

It does look rather nice, doesn't it?

Oh, you look very spunky.

But my head looks like shit. I look like I've got the wrong head.

I like the Calvin Klein underpants.

I look like a real poof. Call that one 'Poof.'

OK, captions simple; no smart-ass, witty captions. This is an art book isn't it? It's not a vulgar merchandising exercise.

Acknowledgments

This book would not have been possible without the creative efforts of many people. It would be churlish of me to miss this opportunity to formally acknowledge those who lent me encouragement, support and, most of all, money.

Thanks are due (in roughly chronological order) to : My family, especially Bruce; The Lesley Parkin Foundation for the Visual Arts; Gabriela Bila; Polly Borland; John Hillcoat; Emma Borland; Anita Lane; Johannes Beck; Peter Gruchot; Nick Fahey; Courtney Pedersen; And of course, Megan Ponsford of Braille Photographics and the silent partners G.R. & G.M.

I would like to dedicate this book to all the girls I've loved before, but it might be better if I narrow it down to a dramatically smaller group – those who loved me back.

PETER MILNE
BERLIN, JULY 1993

Photo of Peter Milne by Katy Beale

Credits

Photos selected and arranged by Mick Harvey & Katy Beale
Text edited by Jessamy Calkin
Layout by Slim Smith
Produced by Rayner Jesson

Duotone origination by La Cromolito, Milan, Italy
Printed and bound in Hong Kong through Palace Press, San Francisco
Production consultant – Endless Graphics

Photographs copyright © Peter Milne
Braille photographics, Melbourne, Australia
Phone 61 3 8247542   Fax 61 3 8248128

Paperback ISBN 0 9522048 5 1
Hardback ISBN 0 9522048 0 0

Originally published by Tender Prey
Ivebury Court, Unit 4, 325 Latimer Rd., London W10 6RA

2.13.61
P.O. BOX 1910 · LOS ANGELES ·
CALIFORNIA · 90078 · USA

2.13.61 PUBLICATIONS / P.O. Box 1910, Los Angeles, CA 90078

OTHER BOOKS FROM 2.13.61:

ROLLINS / See A Grown Man Cry
ROLLINS / Now Watch Him Die
ROLLINS / Black Coffee Blues
ROLLINS / One From None
ROLLINS / Bang!
ROLLINS / Art To Choke Hearts & Pissing In The Gene Pool
JOE COLE / Planet Joe
ALAN VEGA / Cripple Nation
DON BAJEMA / Boy In The Air
BILL SHIELDS / Southeast Asian Book Of The Dead
BILL SHIELDS / Human Shrapnel
NICK CAVE / King Ink
EXENE CERVENKA / Virtual Unreality
EXENE CERVENKA & KEN JARECKE / Just Another War